贝贝熊系列丛书
The Berenstain Bears

THE BIRDS, THE BEES, and the BERENSTAIN BEARS

小鸟，蜜蜂和贝贝熊

当妈妈的膝头再也坐不下了，就说明有件特别的事要发生了……

第一时间的启蒙书

注意这个地方

贝贝熊系列丛书

The Berenstain Bears

THE BIRDS, THE BEES, and the BERENSTAIN BEARS

小鸟，蜜蜂和贝贝熊

(美) 斯坦·博丹　简·博丹　绘著

Stan & Jan Berenstain

孙志芳等　译

父母和孩子一起阅读

家长和子女共同成长

新疆青少年出版社

小熊妹妹有许多事要忙，她对所有的事情都感兴趣。她喜欢看天上的云彩飘来飘去；她喜欢所有粉色的东西；她最喜欢的是她的洋娃娃。她有三个洋娃娃：一个布娃娃，一个丘比娃娃，还有一个能眨眼睛、会喊“妈妈”的婴儿娃娃。

她喜欢各种活动——

她喜欢跑步、跳远、爬高；

她喜欢跳绳；

她还喜欢骑她的三轮车。

小熊妹妹什么都想知道。她想知道天为什么是蓝色的；她想知道星星为什么会眨眼睛；她想知道风是怎么形成的……她突然想起来，这些可以去问问熊爸爸。

一天，当熊妈妈把她抱在腿上读故事的时候，小熊妹妹忽然感到很奇怪：为什么妈妈腿上能坐的地方变小了？

“妈妈！”她喊起来，“你的腿变短了！”

“说得没错。”熊妈妈回答。

“为什么呢？”小熊妹妹继续问。

“你觉得是为什么呢？”熊妈妈反过来问。

“可能是因为你吃的东西太多了。”小熊妹妹一本正经地说。

熊妈妈听了忍不住笑出声来，说：“我可不想吃那么多，真正的原因是——妈妈又有小宝宝了。”

小熊妹妹听明白了。

“哦，妈妈！”

“什么，亲爱的？”

“我们能继续读故事吗？”

“当然。”熊妈妈说着，接着读起了故事。

　　几天以后，小熊妹妹问：“妈妈，小宝宝什么时候出来？”

　　“要好几个月之后吧，”熊妈妈回答说，“知道吗？现在小宝宝还非常小，他正在妈妈身体里一个特别的地方生长。”

　　“什么样的特别的地方？”小熊妹妹很好奇。

　　“我们叫它‘子宫’。”

　　小熊妹妹想了想，说：“听起来和‘屋子’差不多。”

　　“听起来很像，但并不一样。所有的妈妈都会有这个特别的地方，所有的宝宝都在那儿开始生长。”

　　小熊妹妹听明白了。

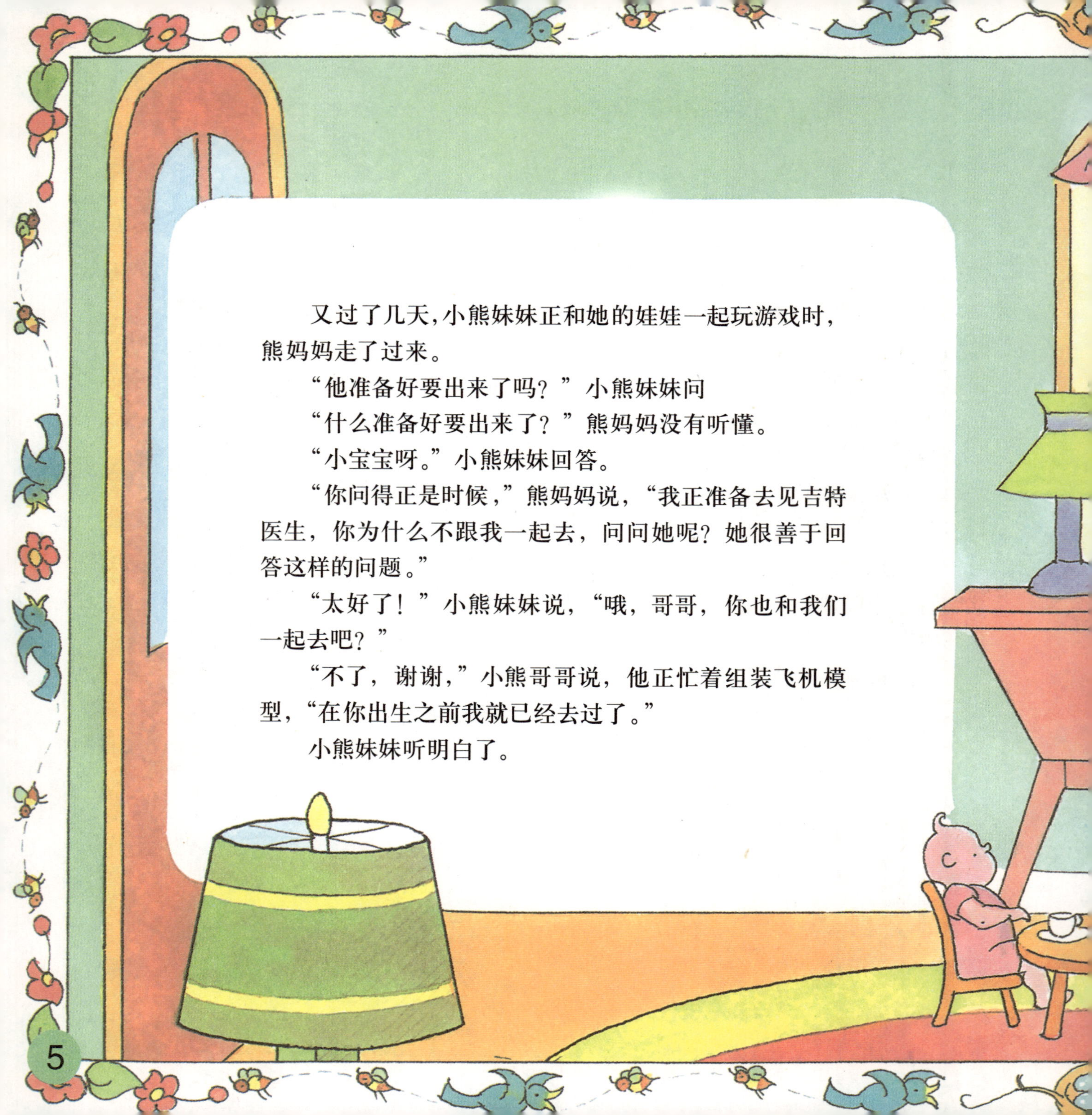

又过了几天，小熊妹妹正和她的娃娃一起玩游戏时，熊妈妈走了过来。

“他准备好要出来了吗？”小熊妹妹问

“什么准备好要出来了？”熊妈妈没有听懂。

“小宝宝呀。”小熊妹妹回答。

“你问得正是时候，”熊妈妈说，“我正准备去见吉特医生，你为什么不跟我一起去，问问她呢？她很善于回答这样的问题。”

“太好了！”小熊妹妹说，“哦，哥哥，你也和我们一起去吧？”

“不了，谢谢，”小熊哥哥说，他正忙着组装飞机模型，“在你出生之前我就已经去过了。”

小熊妹妹听明白了。

“你好，小熊妹妹，”吉特医生说，“很高兴见到你，你知道，你妈妈又要生小宝宝了。见到你我特别高兴，知道吗，你和你哥哥都是我带到这个世界上来的。”

“你是从哪儿把我们带来的呢？”小熊妹妹问。

“噢，那只是用来表达医生帮妈妈们生下小宝宝的一种说法。”吉特医生回答说。

“现在，我要去做检查，看看小宝宝怎么样，你愿意一起来吗？”

小熊妹妹问：“那你怎么检查呢？”

“许多特殊的仪器可以帮我们看到里面的样子，”吉特医生说，“其中一种叫做‘X光机’。”小熊妹妹知道X光，她的脚踝曾经照过X光，用来检查是不是骨折了，不过那次只是扭伤而已。

“这台叫做B超机。”吉特医生说着，将一个像电视遥控器一样的东西放在妈妈肚皮上来回移动。它的一头连着一台大机器，大机器上有一个小小的屏幕，屏幕上显出模糊的图像。

小熊妹妹怎么也看不出来这是小宝宝，但吉特医生肯定能看得出来，因为她不停地在说：“好，不错，非常棒。”

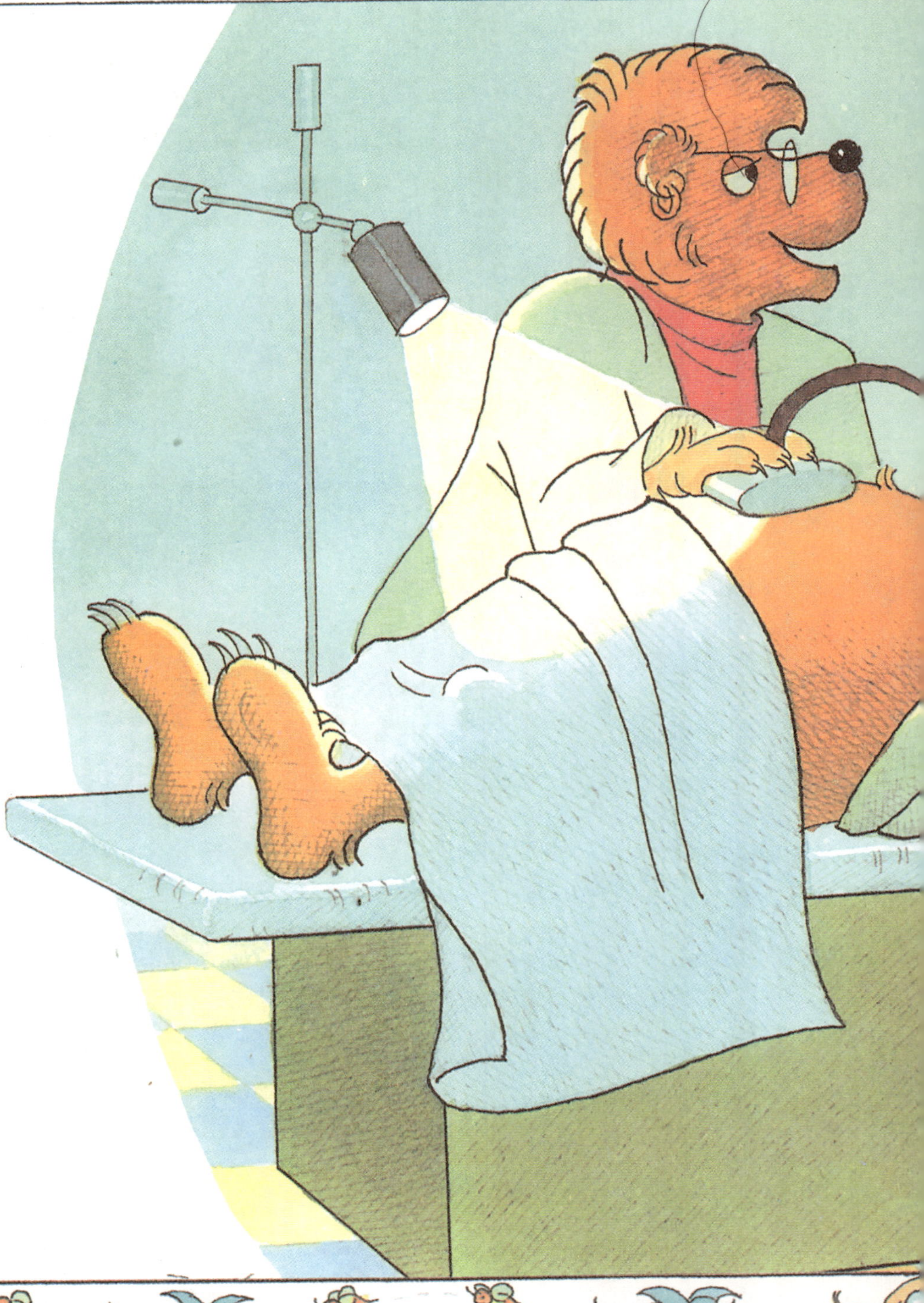

“你妈妈说你有问题要问我？”她们准备离开的时候，吉特医生问小熊妹妹。

“是的，”小熊妹妹说，“小宝宝是怎么生出来的呢？”

吉特医生解释道：“当妈妈和宝宝都做好了准备，小宝宝就会通过妈妈身体里一个负责生产的管道生下来。”

小熊妹妹听明白了。虽然无法想象得十分清楚，但她相信吉特医生，所以她觉得自己明白了，并且接受了这种说法。

她们穿过草地回家时，熊妈妈感叹道：“多美的春天的早晨啊！”那天到处生机盎然：一对知更鸟夫妇正在哺育他们的小宝宝，一只小兔子从她们面前蹦跳着穿过小路。

“看！”熊妈妈指着森林边上的一只鹿说，“看她的肚子多大啊。她和我也许会在同一天生小宝宝呢。”

“看！”小熊妹妹说，“那边有一只长着角的，他会不会是小宝宝的爸爸呢？”

“我想是的。”熊妈妈说。

“天啊——”小熊妹妹说，“好像到处都是小宝宝！”

“好像是这样，”熊妈妈说，“我想你已经注意到那些采花粉的蜜蜂了。”小熊妹妹怎么会注意不到呢？四周到处都是嗡嗡飞舞的蜜蜂。

“这些花儿也会生小宝宝吗？”小熊妹妹问。

“从某方面来说，是的，”熊妈妈回答道，“我想你应该已经注意到了，像小鸟、熊、兔子和鹿都是一出生就能分出性别的。”

“是这样的。”小熊妹妹说。她想起自己和哥哥都还很小的时候，曾经一起洗澡。

“其实，”熊妈妈说，“不仅小鸟和小熊有不同的性别，有些树木和花的性别也是不同的。”

“你是说树和花也能分出男孩和女孩？”

“跟男孩、女孩差不多，”熊妈妈说，“但这只是大概的意思。当蜜蜂采花粉酿蜜的时候，它们也在进行另外一项很重要的工作。它们从花先生那里采集花粉，然后带给花小姐，花小姐就生出许多花的种子，这些种子再开出更多的花。”

小熊妹妹听明白了。

从春天到秋天，熊妈妈胖了一大圈儿，小熊妹妹已经坐不到妈妈的腿上了。

一天早上，熊妈妈对熊爸爸说：“我想是时候了。”于是，熊爸爸打电话给灰熊夫人，她一直负责照看孩子们。灰熊夫人过来照看小熊妹妹和小熊哥哥，熊爸爸则带着熊妈妈去医院，找吉特医生帮助熊妈妈把小宝宝带到这个世界上来。

不久，电话铃响了，是熊爸爸打来的。灰熊夫人接起电话，把话筒递给小熊哥哥和小熊妹妹。“小宝宝已经出生了！”熊爸爸激动地说，“熊妈妈和小宝宝都很好。”

“是男孩还是女孩？”小熊妹妹问，但是熊爸爸已经挂了电话。“爸爸——”小熊妹妹转身对灰熊夫人说：“他没说是弟弟还是妹妹。”

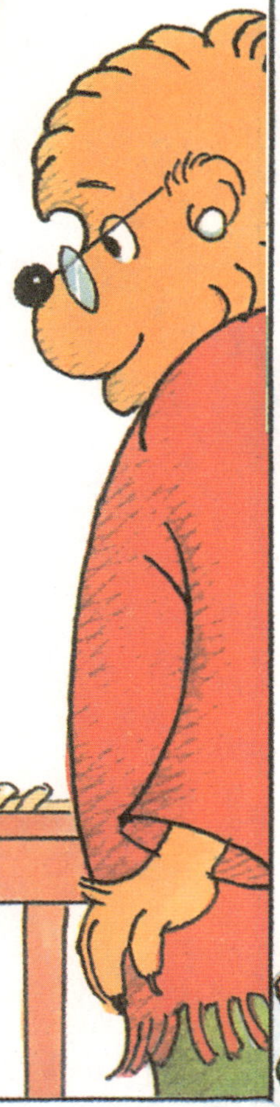

“嗯，”灰熊夫人说，“你爸爸他现在太激动了。他一时忘记了。再说，”她接着说，“最重要的是她们都很平安。”

是的，平安很重要，但其他的事情也很重要。比如：究竟是弟弟还是妹妹？该给他或她起个什么名字呢？小熊妹妹希望是个妹妹，这样她就可以陪自己一起玩洋娃娃什么的；而小熊哥哥则恰恰相反，他希望能有一个弟弟，可以陪自己一起做飞机模型什么的。

事实上，那些事小宝宝都还不会做，不过，他已经会做其他一些事情了。

随后，他们就发现了这一点。小宝宝会哭闹、会扭动、会摇晃、会尿床，还会攥住你的手指头。总有一天，小熊哥哥和小熊妹妹会做的事，他都会做！

小熊妹妹相信这一点。

还有就是——熊妈妈的“腿”又回来了！

The Berenstain Bears

THE BIRDS, THE BEES, and the BERENSTAIN BEARS

When a mama bear's lap slowly disappears, she has some special news to tell her little dears.

1. Sister Bear was a very busy young cub. She liked all different kinds of things. She liked to watch the clouds go by. She liked the color pink. She certainly liked her dolls. She had three of them: a rag doll, a Kewpie doll, and a baby doll that opened and closed her eyes and said, "Mama!"

Sister liked to do all kinds of different things. She liked to run and jump and climb. She liked to jump rope. She liked to ride her trike.

2. Sister wondered about all different kinds of things. She wondered why the sky was blue. She wondered why the stars twinkled. She wondered what made the wind blow. She reminded herself to ask Papa about those things.

One day when Mama took her up onto her lap to read a book, Sister wondered why Mama's lap was getting smaller.

3. "Mama," she said. "Your lap is getting smaller."

"That's true," said Mama.

"Why is that?" asked Sister.

"Why do you suppose?" said Mama.

"Maybe it's because you're eating too much," said Sister.

Mama laughed and said, "I certainly hope not. No, the answer is that I'm going to have a baby."

Sister could accept that.

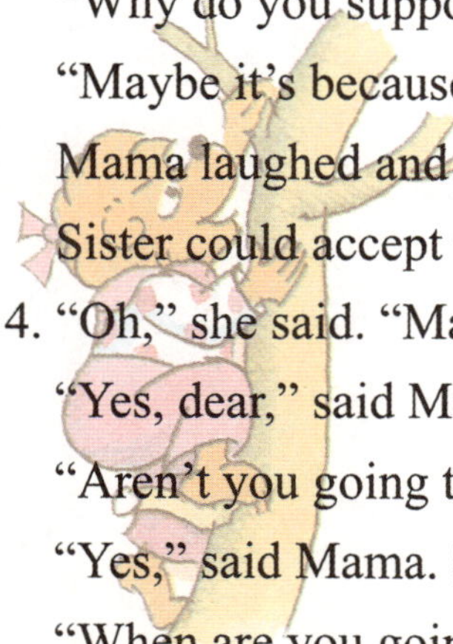

4. "Oh," she said. "Mama?"

"Yes, dear," said Mama.

"Aren't you going to read the book?" said Sister.

"Yes," said Mama. She read the book.

"When are you going to have a baby?" asked Sister a couple of days later.

"Not for many months," said Mama. "You see, the baby is very small now. It's growing in a special place in my body."

"What kind of special place?" asked Sister.

"It's called a 'womb,'" said Mama.

Sister thought about that. "That sounds like 'room,'" sne said.

"*Sounds* like, but *isn't* like," said Mama. "It's a special place that all mamas have where babies can start and grow."

Sister could accept that.

5. A few days later, Sister was playing with her dolls when Mama walked by.

"How's it going to get out?" asked Sister.

"How is *what* going to get out?" asked Mama.

"The baby," said Sister.

"That's a good question," said Mama. "I'm just about to leave for my appointment with Dr. Gert. Why don't you come along and ask her? She's very good at answering questions."

"Okay," said Sister. "Oh, Brother, would you like to come along?"

"No thanks," said Brother, who was in the middle of making a model airplane. "I went through that before you were born."

Sister could accept that.

6."Hello, Sister," said Dr. Gert. "I'm glad to see you. As you know, your mama is going to have another baby. I'm especially glad to see you because I delivered you and your brother."

"Where did you deliver us to?" asked Sister.

"Oh, that's just an expression doctors use for how we help mamas have babies," said Dr. Gert.

"Would you like to come with us? I'm going to have a look and see how the baby's doing."

"How are you going to do that?" asked Sister.

"We have special machines that let us look inside," said the doctor. "One is called an x-ray machine." Sister knew about x-rays. She had her ankle x-rayed once to see if it was broken. But it was just a sprain.

7. “This one is called an ultrasound machine,” said Dr. Gert as she passed a thing that looked like a TV remote over Mama’s tummy. The thing was connected to a big machine that had a little screen. Fuzzy pictures came on the screen. They didn’t look much like a baby to Sister. But they must have to Dr. Gert because she kept saying, “Good. Fine. Excellent.”

8. “Your mama said you had a question for me,” said Dr. Gert as they were about to leave.

“Yes,” said Sister. “How does the baby get out?”

“When the baby and the mama are ready,” explained Dr. Gert, “the baby comes down through a part of the mama’s body called the birth canal.”

Sister could accept that. She couldn’t quite picture it, but she trusted Dr. Gert and she accepted it.

9. “What a beautiful spring morning,” said Mama as they walked home through the meadow. The meadow was very lively that day. A pair of robins were feeding their babies. A baby bunny hopped across their path.

10. “Look!” said Mama, pointing to a deer at the edge of the woods. “See how fat her sides are. She and I might have our babies at the same time.”

“Look!” said Sister. “There’s one with antlers. Do you think maybe he’s the daddy?”

“I think maybe he is,” said Mama.

“Gee,” said Sister. “It looks like babies, babies all over the place!”

“Looks like,” said Mama. “I guess you’ve noticed all the bees visiting the flowers.” How could Sister have helped noticing? The buzz of the busy hovering bees filled the air.

11. “Does that have to do with babies, too?” asked Sister.

“In a way it does,” said Mama. “I guess you’ve noticed that birds and bears and bunnies and deer all come in males and females.”

“Yes,” said Sister. She remembered from when she and Brother were very little and used to take baths together.

“Well,” said Mama, “it’s not just birds and bears that come in males and females. Some trees and flowers do, too.”

"You mean there are boy and girl trees and flowers?"

"More like male and female," said Mama.

"But that's the general idea. And while the honeybees are gathering nectar to make honey, they're doing another important job. They're picking up pollen from the male flowers and carrying it to the female flowers. It's the female flowers that make the seeds that grow into more flowers."

Sister could accept that.

12. Spring grew into summer and summer grew into autumn, and Mama grew to such a size that she had no lap at all.

Then one morning she said to Papa, "I think it's time." Papa called up Mrs. Grizzle, the cubs' regular sitter. She came over to stay with Sister and Brother while Papa took Mama to the hospital, where Dr. Gert would help Mama have the baby.

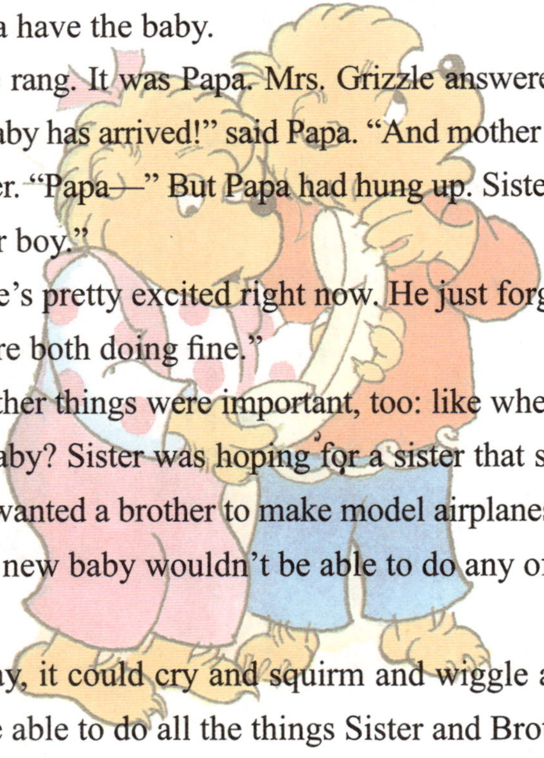

It wasn't long before the phone rang. It was Papa. Mrs. Grizzle answered it. Then she put Sister and Brother on the phone. "The new baby has arrived!" said Papa. "And mother and baby are doing fine!"

"Is it a girl or boy?" asked Sister. "Papa—" But Papa had hung up. Sister turned to Mrs. Grizzle. "He didn't say whether it was a girl or boy."

13. "Well," said Mrs. Grizzle, "he's pretty excited right now. He just forgot. Besides," she continued, "the important thing is that they're both doing fine."

Sure, that was important, but other things were important, too: like whether it was a girl or boy. And what about a name for the new baby? Sister was hoping for a sister that she could play dolls and stuff with. Brother, on the other hand, wanted a brother to make model airplanes and stuff with.

14. But while it was true that the new baby wouldn't be able to do any of those things for some time, it could already do quite a lot.

As they found out later that day, it could cry and squirm and wiggle and wet and even hold on to your finger. Someday it would be able to do all the things Sister and Brother could do.

Sister could accept that.

15. And Mama got her lap back!